THE LEDBURY LAST SUPPER
A Discovery...and a Mystery

An account of the restoration of the painting and
of the circumstances surrounding its creation

by Ronald K. Moore BA Hons Courtauld Institute of Art,
London University • NDD CEd

Published by the Friends of Ledbury Parish Church,
St Michael & All Angels Church, Ledbury, HR8 1PL

© Ronald K. Moore and Patricia Kenny

All rights reserved. No part of this publication may be reproduced,
stored in a retrieval system, or transmitted in any form or by any means,
electronic, mechanical, photocopying, recording, or otherwise
without the prior permission of the publisher.

ISBN 978-0-9558985-2-5

Production and design by Joyce Mason:
joyce@joycemasondesign.com
Copy editing by David Tatham
Cover photograph by Hannah Hiseman
Printed by ABC Print Group, Hereford

TABLE OF CONTENTS

Foreword
— 4 —

Introduction by Ian Beer, CBE,
President of the Friends of Ledbury Parish Church
— 6 —

The Ledbury Last Supper: Lecture by Ronald Moore
— 8 —

Conservation of the Ledbury Last Supper
Notes by the restorer
— 25 —

Appendix to Ronald Moore's Lecture
Notes on Italian Artists of the Renaissance
and text of a minute of 1909 in the Parish Record Book
— 27 —

Thanks and Acknowledgements
— 28 —

FOREWORD

A painting of the Last Supper was presented to Ledbury Parish Church in 1909 and hung, dark and unloved, on the north wall of the Church. When in the summer of 2018 the picture was cleaned and restored the result was a revelation.

This booklet reproduces the lecture which the restorer of the picture, Ronald Moore, delivered when the Ledbury Last Supper was unveiled. We also print some notes by the restorer on the process of conservation and notes on some Italian artists of the Sixteenth Century.

Profits from the sale of this booklet and from illustrations of the Ledbury Last Supper will go to the Friends of Ledbury Parish Church and be devoted to the care and maintenance of the Church.

Work in progress as the restoration of the painting gets underway at Ronald Moore's studio in spring, 2018.

INTRODUCTION

The painting which this booklet describes has hung on a north wall of St Michael & All Angels, the parish church of the market town of Ledbury in Herefordshire, ever since it was donated to the Church in 1909 by Waldyve Martin on behalf of his family which founded Martin's Bank. It was visibly a rendering of the Last Supper but so dark and over-varnished that it aroused little interest and less affection. But early in 2018 the Friends of Ledbury Parish Church received enough encouragement to proceed with the cleaning and restoration of the picture.

Fortunately a restorer equal to the task was ready to hand. In March 2007 Ronald Moore had cleaned the other Last Supper in the church – a copy of Leonardo da Vinci's masterpiece which had been painted by the local artist Thomas Ballard in 1824 and hung over the high altar. At that time he had cleaned a tiny patch of the obscure picture and found bright colours. Now, eleven years later Ronald was prepared to take on this second task of restoration. The picture was lowered from its place on the wall and squeezed into a van which took it to Ronald's studio in a valley close to the border with Wales.

As he worked on the picture Ronald became increasingly enthusiastic. It was clearly by more than one artist, but it was an original and parts, particularly some of the heads of the apostles, were of very high quality. As the work of restoration was completed,

Waldyve Martin (1854-1929).

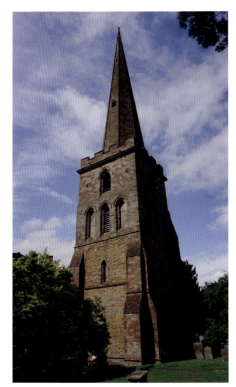

St Michael & All Angels Church, Ledbury.

Ronald used his experience as an art historian from the Courtauld Institute of Art, London University and, assisted by his research assistant Patricia Kenny, endeavoured to discover which artist or artists had created the work. They have traced the plot with the sensibility of artists and the eye for detail of historians and the fruits of their research, 600 hours of it, are set out in the transcript of Ronald Moore's lecture printed here. The picture returned to Ledbury on 1 August 2018. Fresh fixtures had been inserted in the wall and with the help of scaffolding the picture was raised, secured and veiled with a large white tablecloth. On 6 August the Rector of St Michael's, the Reverend Keith Hilton-Turvey, welcomed a large gathering of townsfolk and invited the Bishop of Hereford, the Right Reverend Richard Frith, to unveil the picture. The Bishop cut a tape and the veil fell to the ground: applause for the newly restored Last Supper.

Then the restorer Ronald Moore delivered his lecture on the Ledbury Last Supper, describing his work cleaning and restoring the picture and proposing an attribution. He recounted the story of the painting as a 'most complicated detective story in the field of art' and described a work by several hands, some of them artists of exceptional talent. So, it is thanks to the Friends of Ledbury Parish Church that we owe this exciting outcome – the revelation of a 16th Century Venetian painting of great beauty and real importance. We hope this achievement will encourage more people – church goers and non-churchgoers – to cherish Ledbury's unique church and to join the Friends.

Ian Beer
President of the Friends of Ledbury Parish Church

THE LAST SUPPER c. 1565
ST MICHAEL & ALL ANGELS CHURCH, LEDBURY

This is the text of a lecture given by Ronald Moore, restorer, art historian and artist, on the occasion of the unveiling of the restored Last Supper by the Bishop of Hereford on 6 August 2018.

INTRODUCTION

This large scale painting was probably commissioned as an altarpiece, or a private devotional work in a *palazzo*, and must be totally unique in having been in England for 200 years without ever having been researched or attributed.

Early paintings are rarely what they seem. Most are C18 or C19 copies but this is late Renaissance Venetian. It was almost certainly sent from Venice by John Skippe junior of Upper Hall, Ledbury. He spent much time travelling abroad in the late C18 and in 1775 resided in Venice. He was an artist with some ability in drawing in a C16 Venetian style and the British Museum has a group of his drawings. Skippe was a keen collector of Venetian drawings and is documented as sending paintings back to Upper Hall, one being an altarpiece rolled up but the description of the small size suggests another painting. This was in 1810. He died in 1812 leaving all to his sister, Penelope, who married J. Martin of Overbury Court. Their eldest son Waldyve gave the painting of the Last Supper to St Michael's in 1909 *(see the Parish Record in Appendix)*.

Ledbury Last Supper as the restoration began.

DIFFICULTIES IN ATTRIBUTION

The story of this painting is surely the most complicated detective story in the field of art and has taken me, as an art historian and paintings conservator and my research assistant Patricia Kenny around 600 hours of research. The reason that such a huge painting has never been identified (if it had there would be a record in the church) is because there are many very distinct problems with it.

1 Is it a copy?

At the commencement of restoration it had first to be determined that this was an original painting of the Renaissance, and then that it was not a copy, possibly contemporary but perhaps a version, not a unique work. Many art history books were consulted and thousands of paintings examined from the early 1500s but no painting was discovered that had any relationship. A set of books was obtained from the USA and monographs on Titian, Leonardo, Veronese and Tintoretto studied, together with their drawings.

Then cleaning started to reveal the *pentimenti*. These are changes in the composition made after the initial drawing and cartoon which show through when certain pigments or medium become translucent. The serving boy on the left began to show through the overpaint so was cleaned a little more to make him visible (this was not the artist's intention but fascinating to see and an important discovery). His whole body was painted too and the texture of his garments shown. He was then moved further to the left and another boy added to the right to balance the composition. This figure looks rather cramped. His eyes also show *pentimenti*. as they were clearly moved down to change the shape of the face…

this point will be reconsidered in relation to the influence of Veronese. The second apostle from the right (as you look at the picture, *right*) also has four eyes and the third has three ears as changes were made.

The importance of this lies in the method of transferring a huge drawing onto canvas. The drawing or cartoon was pricked along its lines so that when pressed onto the canvas a bag of charcoal could be pounced over the holes creating lines of dots when the paper, the *spolvero*, was removed. Once this was done only the master could make changes, not an assistant: but in this case it indicates that there was no other version that was being copied. This was an original work, developing as it was created.

2 Smalt

Smalt (*smaltino* in Italian) was finely ground blue glass and a by-product of the Venetian glass industry. Seemingly it was a wonderful discovery since azurite and lapis lazuli (only obtained, then as now, from Afghanistan) were the only other blues apart from the newly found indigo (used in dyes) available in Venice. Lapis cost more than gold and azurite was often lacking in intensity so smalt seemed perfect.

The glass was mixed with linseed or walnut oil, the latter forming wide cracks on drying, and sometimes also with ground clear glass to speed the drying process (cf the boy on right). What they did not know was that in time the blue faded to brown in oil, completely changing the colour balance of the painting. When mixed with lead white smalt is protected. The fourth apostle from the right would be a rich ultramarine as would the fifth from the left. The two serving boys comprise indigo and smalt with malachite in walnut oil and the wonderful man

with a dark beard certainly had shadows on his garment which have now gone, probably from careless restoration long ago. He would have looked more purple than the probable red of the madder plant which is still there.

So imagine the composition with a blaze of rich blues across it. We now begin to see the influence of Titian rather than Leonardo alone. We see rich, varied, powerful, colours, carefully balanced.

This 'Titian Last Supper' (1542-1544) shows many links with ours – the basic elongated table with a figure either end; figure grouping; the boy with platter; the reclining John; the dog; floor tiles; and the psychological drama.

The perspective of the lines on the floor emphasizes the Christ figure and interestingly the vanishing point is on Christ's chest not his forehead as in Leonardo's, nor on his neck as in the Ledbury Last Supper.

3 Venice

The art market in Venice in the *cinquecento* (C16) is, surprisingly, very little understood. There were very many schools and intersections between them. The audiences were varied, the commissions came from various sources and the links between the master painters were more frequent than we imagine. There is much information on Titian, Veronese and Tintoretto but almost nothing on the huge amount of workshops influenced by them. Even a recent major exhibition on the school and followers of Titian consisted mainly of paintings which were not attributed.

4 Painters involved
Looking at the heads of the apostles there are clearly some six painters involved. Some are notably weaker than others but the four apostles with white/grey beards, (*right*, described as 'the greybeards' from now on) are of remarkable quality, as are the two figures on the left. The question now arises: why are there such variations in ability?

5 Lack of signature
Rarely are paintings of this period signed.

THE SOURCES OF THE STYLE

1 Veronese and Venice
Initially the influences on the painting seemed to be from Paolo Caliari, known as Veronese. The two page boys/servants were surely influenced by the two figures in doorways in the Veronese fresco at the Villa Barbaro whilst the boy on the right is remarkably like the boy in his 'Feast in the House of Levi'. (It was common for Veronese to include in his paintings young boys aged 10-12 who were beginning their training as assistants.)

Then there were the wide range of colours, typical of Veronese and now available in Venice. This will be described further below.

I then found one drawing by Veronese which showed a rear window and three lateral windows much like our painting which was a further clue to some involvement with a school related to Veronese. The whole composition is not, of course, Mannerist

[3]

The figures in square brackets denote the position of the seated apostles, numbering from the left.

[5]

[6]

[9]

and is not typical of Veronese. Further research proved that Benedetto Caliari, Veronese's brother, painted the architectural backgrounds for his brother's paintings, which were complex Palladian in style. This led towards the '*Haeredes Pauli*', (the heirs of Paolo), the followers and family of the great workshop of the master but then an examination of the PhD thesis of an Italian scholar (Thomas da Costa of Verona University) showed again that the *Haeredes* were not responsible.

2 Leonardo da Vinci

At first glance our painting bears some similarity to Leonardo's 'Last Supper' fresco in Santa Maria delle Grazie, Milan (1495-98), until we consider the missing blues in our picture. The format is similar, with the long table and no figures seen from the back. The simple architecture also emphasizes the figures and in our picture the vanishing point for the lateral windows is on a point on Christ's neck (Leonardo's is on his forehead) and a tiny hole is still visible filled with a speck of cochineal where our artist stuck a pin and extended strings to the windows to create his vanishing point and perspective lines.

Venetian painters were aware of the Leonardo, completed almost a century earlier, as a relief sculpture of his 'Last Supper' by Tullio Lombardo was in Venice.

The figure groupings are also similar in part and Peter's gesture, to the left of Christ in our painting and to the right in Leonardo, is similar.

3 Titian

Titian's several last suppers bear a strong resemblance to our painting although he uses more tonal contrasts and dramatic shadow. Our Last Supper shows the same psychological realism, close observation of types and range of types, in part, as do Titian's and Leonardo's work. Titian did not die until 1576 and his influence continued throughout the century.

PIGMENTS

So the varied influences on our painting prove its Venetian, certainly Veneto (the region around Venice), source. Many of the pigments relate also to Venice.

The dye trade had developed the use of smalt, indigo and powdered glass.

(The two boys are painted in smalt indigo and the green stripes are malachite in walnut oil). The sky is comprised of verdigris mainly in linseed oil and the darks are azurite indigo and smalt with lead white. Some parts are mixed with lead white which has protected the blues but these are limited. The dark clouds have darkened considerably and were once a rich dark blue.

The third apostle from the right (possibly Judas, although he is not knocking over the salt cellar which iconographically he often does) has a base colour of orange ochre with overpaint of orpiment (the orange yellows) and a tiny line of lead tin yellow to the right.

[11] *Figure in orange yellows, thought possibly to be Judas.*

[13] *Detail of dark red cloak.*

The dark reds of the cloaks are mainly cochineal (pressed insects), and kermes, (which is another insect). There is also madder: rose madder (*rubia tinctorum*) which is now known as alizarin crimson but was then paler and it is probably on the second apostle on the left. He seems to lack shadows and would certainly have had some on his cloak. I believe smalt may have been used in a thin glaze here and that a careless cleaning long ago removed the glazes.

CANVAS

A horizontal line may be seen running along the table cloth (the detailed edging is typical of Venetian cloths as is the tiled floor). This is due to the fact that looms were only around 40 inches (107mm) or so. Veronese's canvas was 39 inches (99mm) and ours is 44 inches (117mm). The two pieces were sewn together and over the centuries it is common to find that the thread has degraded and the pieces are becoming split. This is usually solved by lining, i.e. adhering the old canvas to a new one. (This can be done by ironing from the back using, in the past, animal glue. From the 1950s a vacuum lining table was often used with heat activated adhesive which is reversible).

Detailed edging along the tablecloth and the tiled floor are typical of Venetian style of this period.

This painting was lined c 1800 with a vegetable or animal based glue and I believe a local carpenter made a new stretcher. This is very strong with one central stretcher bar but does not have expandable mitres on the corners which could take up loose canvas as the tension in the fabric changes.

ATTRIBUTION

After some 300 hours of research, it was now becoming clear that we had a Venetian painting, possibly commissioned as a church altarpiece, although it could have been for a palazzo, produced by a workshop other than one of the three major ones. Given the Veronesian influences a 'satellite' of his seemed likely but all painters were also being influenced by Titian at the time and our painting has stronger Titianesque features than Veronesian.

I next looked at many hundreds of paintings, some not even attributed, to try to find similarities of any sort. I considered several possible artists. A good choice seemed Alvise dal Friso (Luigi Benfatto) many of whose compositions recalled Titian but who was also Veronese's nephew. However he only signed one painting.

Francesco Montemezzano was another possibility although his work was finer and richer in colour.

Bonifacio d'I Pitati (Bonifacio Veronese) was another assistant to Titian.

Paris Bordone was also a possibility but had a quite different style.

Now, Polidoro da Lanciano was one of Titian's four main assistants for many years. He was also less Veronesian with more a feel of Titian. In fact a number of 'Titians' have now been attributed instead to Polidoro. Polidoro's work is quite varied in quality but he has only one documented painting and his 'work' is mainly attributions and opinions. It is likely that he ran a small studio although there is no documentation on this and he also had two children who almost certainly continued his work.

Veronese pen ink and wash study with similar use of lateral windows with light shining through to the right.
Staatlichte Museum

Detail of Veronese fresco at Villa Barbaro. The novel idea of 'our' serving boys in large architectural doorways surely has its precedent here.

NB There are no signed paintings by Polidoro and the 'Pentecost' (Venice Accademia 415) completed in 1545 and recorded by Vasari as by Bonifazio Veronese, is his only dated work. There is a strong influence of Titian in the 'Pentecost'. Some early research suggests his late 1520s work may be placed in Titian's workshop.

Our painting is not all typical of the work of Polidoro however because of the many hands involved, some five or six I believe, which range in quality from wonderful to indifferent, as is particularly evident in the heads. A slight variation of style is not unusual given that in a large workshop like that of Veronese there were many assistants and pupils working on huge canvasses. Our heads however show quite different styles and abilities, so the question now was: why had this occurred? What explains all the anomalies?

PROPOSAL FOR WORKING PROCESS

I propose that Polidoro da Lanciano worked out his composition in the normal high Renaissance manner, with individual drawings of heads and figures, groupings of figures, a cartoon and *spolvero* transfer to canvas in 1564. In this year he made his will and was ill and I propose that at this point, whilst he had accepted the commission, he was not able to fulfil it all. He may have painted some of the well-drawn heads although not the four outstanding ones (the 'greybeards') nor the two on the left. It seems unlikely, if my idea is right, that he would have painted the drapery, which is lacking in quality in some places. This would have been completed by his children and studio after his death in 1565. It is even possible that Polidoro did not actually work on the canvas in paint, but rather prepared the composition as described.

How can we be sure of this? Well, we cannot since I have examined all the documents in Italian on Polidoro that I could trace (some fourteen), and there is no evidence of how our painting was commissioned, executed and where it was sited originally (The Hereford/Ledbury archives have also proved to have no related documents although we do know that John Skippe and the Martin family had more documents than we saw relating to his sending paintings from Venice, but these have disappeared. They would surely have named the church or palazzo from whence it was bought).

So returning to the problematic aspects of this attribution:

1 The *pentimenti*
We looked at these earlier and saw the importance of the fact that they exist at all. The changes probably indicate the presence of a new master painter. The background between the serving boy and first apostle with the 'floating head', the *pentimento*, appears to have been painted over at the same time as the architectural interior was painted. This gives us some idea of the order in which the parts were completed. The two boys are painted in quite a different technique using a green earth underpaint with warm pigments over but allowing some cool colour to show through. This is the only place in the picture where this method is used and indicates another hand again.

It also creates the question as to why they were added and by whom, given that they surely relate to Veronese's two figures in doorways in his fresco. Does this suggest another hand who worked in Veronese's studio?

The two serving boys are by the same artist but the pentimento 'floating head' (left) is by a quite different hand and is freely executed, more in the style of the 'grey-beards'. It has a somewhat menacing quality and must be a portrait. Again we see he has red hair.

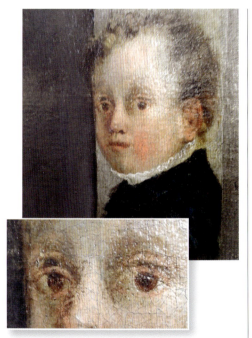

The boy (above) added to the right hand side of the painting, showing pentimenti. The eyes have been moved further down to change the shape of the face as the detail below clearly shows.

My proposal for the working is that perhaps after Polidoro died there were only parts completed, a few heads and perhaps some of the table items. The 'studio' then continued work as best they could since the patron would want their picture:

2 The six heads. (1, 2, 3, 5, 6 and 9 counting from the left)

Who were possibly the two master painters who then came to help? The style of the four similar heads (the 'greybeards' 3, 5, 6, 9) is quite unlike, say, the heads of Christ and John although the four apostles to the right of Christ are highly competent. Then the two heads to the left (1 and 2) are remarkable in quality but somewhat different again in brushwork from the four.

The man with the dark beard bears a close resemblance to what Tintoretto would look like around seventeen years after his well-documented self-portrait of 1548. He is obviously a portrait executed with remarkable observation as he looks out directly at us. This fact of his looking directly at the viewer is highly significant. Painters often included themselves in a group of figures and if our face is that of a middle-aged Tintoretto then would it be surprising? Polidoro and Tintoretto possibly worked in Titian's studio together. In fact Tintoretto did not find Titian agreeable since the latter made Tintoretto paint versions of his work. It seems Tintoretto possibly stayed with Titian for only a short time as a result although there is little documentation of the dates other than Ridolfi in 1648.

Are the two wonderful heads Tintoretto and someone else obviously significant? Is the man with the black beard a self-portrait or perhaps a portrait of Tintoretto by some other master painter? The man on his left looks somewhat like the few images we have of Veronese at this age in his masterpiece 'The Feast in the House of Levi'.

These two heads appear superimposed and clearly their garments were painted by a studio hand whilst the four old men (the 'greybeards' 3, 5, 6 and 9) have a beautiful freedom of brushwork, light and character which speaks of a major painter. It seems unlikely that Polidoro could have painted them.

We have so little information on the movement between studios within Venice and even on a world basis. El Greco came to Venice at this point and worked in some studios. Titian was known to add heads and hands to the work of various artists and several Dutch painters are also documented.

In my opinion we clearly have a great painter involved but there is such a lack of documentary evidence and research on this period that one can only make considered decisions based on comparison with other paintings. Movements between studios certainly took place but little is written on this. An art dealer might perhaps make robust statements on attribution when selling but an art historian requires documentation if possible, yet so little exists, particularly without spending a considerable time in Venice or the Vatican Archives.

OUTSIDE OPINIONS

At this point some 600 hours had been undertaken and one had to look to acknowledged experts in each particular field of this work. This is the way to

[1] *This head (the second figure from the left of our painting) is clearly a portrait and of very high quality. It is most likely to be a Venetian nobleman a patron or the portrait of an artist. It does have some similarities to Veronese himself (see portraits opposite).*

Veronese self-portrait in 'The Feast in the House of Levi', 1573.

Detail of a self-portrait of Titian as a young man.

achieve a successful attribution. Two world-class auction houses and their old master departments were consulted, as were the leading British expert and writer on Venetian painting, the director of a leading old master gallery in the USA and expert on Veronese and Tintoretto, a leading Italian art historian on the *Haeredes Pauli* and Professor Alessandra Zamperini from Verona University, author of the major work on Veronese and expert on the period. All expressed great interest and excitement but none solved the mystery of the canvas of our Last Supper.

Professor Zamperini stated that sometimes, given the lack of research one simply has to give up but I then sent her my proposal for an attribution for the workshop of Polidoro da Lanciano. Professor Zamperini replied:

> I think that your idea may be a good solution in my personal opinion. I would support Polidoro da Lanciano, the less Veronesian, you are right, and the most known… given that no one has so far been able to decipher your painting. This mysterious canvas is rooted in the Venetian culture however it does not belong to any hand we are acquainted with without doubt (i.e. indisputably).
>
> I suggest you stick to Polidoro as the most plausible option so far. Your reconstruction of the working process involved is original and very sensible. I was positively surprised when you described it to me.
>
> I support your opinion… and think that your proposal of Polidoro's painting being completed after his death appropriate. Titianesque hands being involved are a good interpretation.

NB Professor Zamperini's opinions only relate to Polidoro and the process whereby the painting was created.

FINAL PROPOSAL OF ATTRIBUTION

I believe that we may have an undocumented 'workshop painting' (i.e. not autograph) by Polidoro da Lanciano who was ill and dying in 1564 when he wrote his will, dying a year later. He completed the early work on the painting, the drawings, cartoon etc and perhaps some parts before he died. His family and possibly a studio then needed help to complete the commission and were helped by two painters.

Could these have been major assistants from Tintoretto's workshop or even Tintoretto himself. There is some similarity of brushstroke, style and facial types/models with the four greybeards and the fact of the two painters probably once working together would be encouraging.

There are also many features in the painting which link it to Veronese and Titian as we have seen. As yet there is no documentation linking our painting with any other workshop but there is no doubt that this link existed and that the hands behind the 'greybeards' and the two portraits were those of a painter of note.

It should be noted that in this context 'workshop assistants' often became major painters in their own right with considerable influence (e.g. Paris Bordone in Titian's shop and Bonifazio Veronese in Veronese's shop).

Also to note is the fact that the many Titianesqe features in our Last Supper are now leading the research into a closer look at not just the connection between Polidoro and Titian but Tintoretto's later link with Titian`s workshop and that of his son Domenico Tintoretto.

[2] *The man with the black beard, second apostle from the left: a superb portrait by a noted, but as yet, unknown artist, bearing some resemblance to what Tintoretto would look like 17 years after his self-portrait (opposite).*

Tintoretto self-portrait, 1548.

CONCLUSION

Given the total lack of documents on our Last Supper so far (although we are pursuing sources in England now) nor any comparable painting it is impossible for anyone to be definitive on this mysterious canvas. Six major art historians have reached no conclusion but one has agreed with our proposal of Polidoro and the possible creation of the work.

I believe this painting may be tentatively attributed to Polidoro da Lanciano, Titian's assistant, to his studio and probably two other important painters, possibly Polidoro's old friend, Tintoretto, was involved or some of his major assistants although only working on four of the heads.

I have examined all the documents on Polidoro available to me at this time (some with thanks to the scholar Dr Vincenzo Mancini) and there is no reference to a Last Supper (a subject common to almost all painters at this time and especially those so strongly influenced by Titian and Veronese).

I think therefore that this Ledbury Last Supper may be the lost Last Supper of Polidoro da Lanciano… and friends.

POST SCRIPT

Given the limited amount of previous research on the period, documents, or signatures, over the years there have been many disputes and changes in attribution with many painters. There is still much to be learnt about this painting and in time more documentation and knowledge may emerge. Positive identification of 'the heads' will be an important discovery.

Any alternative attribution would have to explain the anomalies of style and quality together with documentation.

Further investigation will especially concentrate on the original documentation in Venice and England and more technical analysis. A comparison *(right)* between one of our heads and a Tintoretto (Yale University Library Art Gallery 2015.138.1) shows some obvious similarities of brushwork and technique but the pigments in both are the same. Various red earth colours, ochre, black and white lead with a dark ground.

It is interesting that despite the many colours now available in Venice due to the dye trade and whilst Tintoretto often used all these throughout a painting, his faces were often reduced to earth colours although this was together with a more linear emphasis not seen in our four heads. He could have included lac lakes (from cochineal and kermes) and vermilion as well as realgar and orpiment for orange tints.

One has to wonder if glazes are missing from our faces, lost in poor old cleaning techniques.

This surely all indicates that our visiting artist was well-acquainted with the techniques used in Tintoretto's workshop.

Closer examination of materials and pigments, techniques and movements between the workshops of Veronese, Titian and Tintoretto together with further documentation on Polidoro and the source of the painting will be future lines of exploration. We shall continue the research.

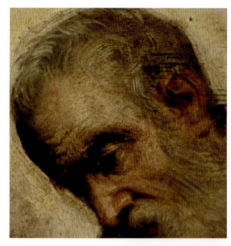

Since delivering this lecture, Ronald Moore has come across a head by Tintoretto (above) which bears a marked resemblance to one of the 'greybeards' (right) – [5] from the left in the Ledbury Last Supper. This head is a detail in Tintoretto's 'Holy Family with the young St John', of 1547 in the Yale University Art Gallery.

The dog beneath the table in the Ledbury Last Supper shows similarities to dogs from paintings by Veronese (below) and Titian (bottom).

CONSERVATION OF THE LEDBURY LAST SUPPER
Notes by the restorer, Ronald Moore

The many weeks of work which I devoted to this work with the complex processes and chemical details cannot be adequately described briefly. But this is an outline of some of the work involved.

The conservation consisted of, primarily, six parts:

1 Close examination and photography, recto and verso, then removal of accumulated dust and dirt behind the canvas.

2 Surface cleaning: this removes surface dirt, dust, spillages, grease etc so that a less powerful solvent may be used in the next stage. Pastes and gels with adjustable alkaline properties were used and were carefully monitored for pH level and neutralized afterwards on the painting. (Water which degrades glue binders on the canvas and may cause flaking was not used).

3 Removal of the C18 mastic varnish (a soft resin varnish which may be dissolved by solvents). The appropriate solvents were tested on many pigments and areas of the paint surface, some pigments being more fugitive or painted in a glaze medium. This assessed the safety of the process, the aim being to remove the varnish as quickly as reasonably possible without any damage with a solvent which then vaporizes rapidly, reducing further unwanted action. The various solvents were mixed with white spirit or turpentine to reduce them.

4 Removal of old retouching/overpaint. Ultra-violet fluorescence showed that there were many areas which had been overpainted and this had to be removed using stronger solvents and a scalpel in places. The clouds especially had been

completely retouched in black as had the *pentimenti* relating to the two serving boys. I removed the black clouds to reveal dark indigo and some smalt although this would have been far richer in its original colour. (Mixing with linseed oil had darkened the smalt which partially turned dark brown although the effect was mitigated by the addition of some azurite and the indigo.) The decision was made to leave the changes to the boy on the right and other figures and particularly the 'floating head' on the left. This was not the artists' intention of course but they reveal important changes in the composition as it developed. There were many other various retouchings removed.

5 Filling damage and paint losses and the long gap where the two pieces of canvas had disengaged; and retouching to match existing colours. This was completed with artists' pigments and synthetic resin. Loose paint was reaffixed with wax and a hot spatula.

The background architecture was in very bad condition with many abrasions and paint losses, probably from poor cleaning techniques in the past and a considerable amount of retouching was required since the tonalities had changed from dark to light in many places as a lighter paint ground was revealed by the damage. There were several holes, tears and extensive paint losses lower left, on the right along the lower edge and along the entire join on the table cloth. The faces, fortunately, had almost no losses or damage. The extensive damage to the lower edge and left end suggest that the painting stood on a floor for a considerable time with objects leaning against it.

6 Finally warm varnish was applied by use of a compressor and spray gun.

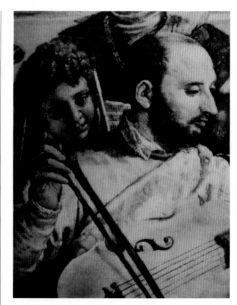

Self-portrait of Veronese as a musician in his painting of 'The Feast in the House of Levi'. Note the figure of the boy behind with curly hair (which is in fact red).

Restorer Ronald Moore varnishing the Ledbury Last Supper outside his studio in Herefordshire.

APPENDIX (*to Ronald Moore's lecture*)

SOME ITALIAN ARTISTS OF THE RENAISSANCE

Leonardo da Vinci 1452-1519

A painter of genius (and architect, sculptor, engineer and scientist) he completed his 'Last Supper' in 1498 in the church of Santa Maria delle Grazie, Milan. The version over the high altar in St Michael & All Angels is a copy by the local artist Thomas Ballard dating from 1824.

Titian c.1490-1576

(in Italian *Tiziano Vecellio*). Born in Pieve di Cadore in the Veneto, he is widely considered the greatest of the Venetian painters.

Polidoro da Lanciano 1515-1565

Born in Lanciano in central Italy he moved to Venice in the 1530s to work as a painter and was for a time an assistant to Titian. Eight of his paintings with religious subjects are in British galleries.

Tintoretto 1518-94

Born Jacopo Robusti, the son of a dyer (*tintore*), he lived almost all his life in Venice. He painted spectacular murals on sacred subjects.

Veronese 1528-1588

Born Paolo Caliari in Verona (hence his name) he settled in Venice and painted large works. These include 'The Feast in the House of Levi' (1573) which brought him before the Inquisition for his irreverent treatment of a religious subject. His brother Benedetto Caliari also painted.

Extract from the Vestry Record Book of Ledbury Parish Church

Held in the Herefordshire Archive and Records Centre.

> We, the Rector and Churchwardens of Ledbury Parish Church have received from Mr Martin of the Upper Hall, as a gift to the Church, the picture of 'The Last Supper' believed to be 'after Titian'. In presenting the picture to the Church Mr Martin makes it a condition that if ever it is removed from the Church it will be returned to him or his heirs and this condition is accepted by us.
>
> Fred. W. Carnegy (*Rector*)
> Cuthbert Bastow, Frederick Wm. Taylor (*Churchwardens*),
> May 27, 1909

ACKNOWLEDGEMENTS

The Friends of Ledbury Parish Church wish to thank the following people and companies who made the restoration and re-installation of the Ledbury Last Supper possible: Ronald Moore, restorer and art historian, and Patricia Kenny his assistant.

The benefactors who funded the restoration.
Shane Howells Builders who installed the restored painting.
Brandon plant hire.
Ian Stainburn.

They are also grateful for the constant support and encouragement of the Rector, the Reverend Keith Hilton-Turvey.

...tances where we have been unable to trace or contact the copyright holder. If notified the ...ll be pleased to rectify any errors or omissions at the earliest opportunity.

Brandon Goodwin of Shane Howells Ltd steadies the painting during its re-hanging.